THE PRACTICAL
T̲O̲ CRYS'
HEALI̲N̲G̲

Gemcraft Books

GEMCRAFT BOOKS
291-293 Wattletree Road, East Malvern,
Vic., 3145, Australia

*This book is copyright.
Apart from any fair dealings for the
purposes of private study, research,
or review, as permitted under
the Copyright Act, no part may be
reproduced by any process without
written permission of the publisher.*

*Copyright © Marc James & Dhyan Klein
National Library of Australia
Cataloguing-in-publication data.
James, M. & Klein, D
The Practical Guide to Crystal Healing
ISBN O 909223 96 3*

*Cover design and illustration by
Dessein, Perth, W.A.*

*1st Printing - November 1988
2nd Printing - March 1989
3rd Printing - November 1989
4th Printing - September 1990
5th Printing - February 1991*

*Printed in Australia
by Globe Press.*

CONTENTS

ABOUT THE AUTHORS

MARC JAMES -Trained as a scientist with an honours degree in computers and cybernetics Marc simultaneously explored the mysteries of human consciousness through Tarot, philosophy and yogic techniques. Travels in the East brought him into contact with Indian and Tibetan Masters who turned those intellectual ideals into living reality and hence changed the course of his life.

Since then he's used his scientific awareness to explore many more new age techniques and extract the practical essence of them. For the last 5 years crystals have been the prime focus of his life because after so many years in so many different systems of consciousness and lifestyle the simple down to earth clarity of these stones became the perfect focus.

Now living in Melbourne, Australia, Marc runs a popular New Age crystal shop and looks forward to writing a series of books on his different areas of interest.

DHYAN KLEIN - Dhyan is one of those rare people born with an incredible energy for life which led her to leave her comfortable upbringing at an early age and launch herself into many experiences now known collectively as the New Age.

Travelling the world to work with Indian and Tibetan Zen masters, psychics and healers, she was one of the first western women allowed to study Tibetan Temple dancing. Trained in rebirthing, past life regression, reiki healing, colour therapy, psychodrama and psychic development to name but a few areas, she has always focused her energies on healing by whatever means appropriate. She has been running popular workshops which integrate all these areas for the last 11 years. Eight years ago she was intuitively led to her first crystals which opened up a whole new dimension for her, and since that time they have been the central theme in all her work.

INTRODUCTION

Welcome to the world of crystals. We hope that the following words, in which we've literally "crystallised" many years of experience with these wonderful stones, will give you a clear idea of what crystals are all about, what they can do for you, and how to use them. The Practical Guide to Crystal Healing contains all essential knowledge and techniques needed to work with crystals successfully.

Since Ancient times, man has intuitively recognised and acknowledged the beneficial effects of all types of gemstones, but most particularly those of Natural Quartz Crystal. The versatility, clarity and energy properties of this stone earned it the title "King of the Mineral World", and make it a worthy focus for this book.

In more recent times all our focus has been on developing the rational organised scientific mind and this has led to a tremendous transformation of our physical existence. But in the process we've lost touch with those intuitive abilities which "primitive" man had developed to a much greater degree, and so we've lost our balance. The tremendous growth in popularity of crystals in recent years simply reflects the necessary resurgence of that ancient way of knowing.

Working with clear quartz crystal stimulates the innate intelligence which we all possess and which breathes so much life and enjoyment into our everyday reality. Crystals have always exerted this almost magical fascination on the human psyche because they speak both to the head and the heart, and in so doing integrate both the rational and intuitive sides of our being.

Throughout history, one thing has been recognised about these stones. Crystals are Healers. Somehow their natural beauty and symmetry and the particular quality of light they carry, means that wherever and however crystals are used, they heal. Crystals can be used in so many ways; to expand your psychic or intuitive abilities and hence work with energy and vision; they can be used for meditation; they're wonderful tools for creative visualisation and can be programmed to facilitate achievement of our goals. Through crystals we can heal ourselves and others, bringing greater clarity and fulfilment into our lives.

In all this we can't underestimate the power of our intuition. After all, it is an intuitive leap which actually precedes every scientific breakthrough or the creation of anything new in our society. Crystals can be seen as a bridge from our apparently fixed physical world into another level of existence from which we can create a new reality. We all know this space, we've simply forgotten it in the daily grind of our lives.

It's not surprising that quartz does have some interesting physical properties which help to explain why it, in particular, is special. When squeezed, for example, it emits an electromagnetic energy field. Scientists call this the piezo electric effect and it accounts for the extensive use of crystal in the electronics and computer industries - also great transformers of our lives!

Psychics have also long known that our physical body carries its own electromagnetic field or aura, and further that this does indicate the physical, mental, emotional and spiritual state of health of each individual. A long tradition of psychic healers have known that the energy field of clear quartz can interact with that of the human body in a positive manner.

The problem has always been that scientists can't see what psychics can. Until, that is, the invention of the Kirlian Camera.

6

This remarkable device actually photographs the aura and shows that it does indeed indicate many dimensions of the state of health of each individual. Some American hospitals have been using it experimentally as a diagnostic tool with very promising results.

Putting these things together we can see through Kirlian photography that when someone holds a clear quartz crystal then their energy field is intensified, and it's this effect which forms the basis of crystal healing. Of course, the energies involved are physically very suble; yet because we're working so much closer to the source the results can be amazing.

So welcome again to the world of crystals. Before we go more into the healing techniques, we'll talk a little about how to choose, care for, and connect to your crystals.

HOW CRYSTALS ARE FORMED

Most of us have already seen natural quartz crystal at some time in our lives, probably in the form of a "Single Terminator" which is a six sided clear crystal with the top facets coming to a point. These can be so perfectly formed that it's often hard to believe they're actually created by nature and not by man. Even after so many years working with these stones this is a continual source of wonder.

Crystals are also found in clusters - a group or family of single terminators sharing a common base, and more rarely as double terminations where a crystal has been able to grow a point at both ends. All these different forms have different uses but in this book we'll focus on the single terminators as these are by far the most versatile to work with.

Crystals are formed when superheated steam escapes from the magma underlying the Earth's crust through natural fissues in it. These fissures allow space for the minerals carried by the steam to crystallise out on the walls in the perfect shapes we're familiar with. The point about these crystals and the reason why they all form the same familiar six sided shape is that the component molecules aren't arranged in a haphazard manner but instead have a definite ordered structure. In the case of quartz, every crystal is made up from a geometrically precise spiral of silicon and oxygen atoms held together by jointly shared electrons.

It's this structure which explains the electrical properties that we mentioned in the introduction, for when mechanical pressure is applied (it's squeezed, for example) then the electrons nearest the surface are displaced inwards and upwards through the helix to be emitted mainly through the point. Then when the pressure is released the crystal simply recharges by absorbing free electrons from the air.

This flow of electrons through the crystal, combined with its ability to resonate with, amplify, and transmute your own personal energy input, gives a very clear picture of how crystal can be such a powerful and positive energy tool for working on the human mind, body, and soul.

The crystals that you can buy or find are generally very old. It's quite fair to talk of ages up to millions of years. But it's also important to remember that they are being formed all the time. Crystals are part of the continuous process of life and evolution of the mineral world on this planet, and so I don't find it strange (any more!) to talk in terms of 'Mineral Life'. After all crystals have a common form, just as we do. Within that general form each is an individual and each has energy flowing through, just like you and me. And in that helical spiral, which is such a universal symbol, I see the familiar echoes of our own D.N.A., of spiral galaxies and more. So it's good to know when you pick up a crystal that you're connecting not only to the Earth but also to yourself, and to the Universe you live in.

It seems to me that the great age of crystals must be a factor in their transformational properties. After all, consider how strongly one can feel the presence of an ancient tree or building; of something born or built in an age of man now lost in time. Crystals are unimaginably older, and in their long lives have absorbed and recorded so many changes in the Earth and the Universe it spins in. Whilst such speculation is a little off the track for this book, it's well worth exploring; particularly through the visualisation techniques given later.

CHOOSING CRYSTALS

The main point in choosing a crystal is to trust your own impulsive intuitive attraction. This means that I'll often pass over an apparently perfect crystal which does nothing for me in favour of a less perfect one which just feels right. It has some quality to which part of me is attracted and so I know I can learn something from it. Crystals are just like people - one can't always tell by appearances!

Nevertheless, in choosing crystals for healing it is important to choose a crystal which has good clarity and a good unchipped point. So, having selected a few prospects the next step is to tune in to each one individually and find the one that's right for you.

To do this hold the crystal in your left hand, point inward. Relax a little, allowing your attention to be drawn away from the environment outside and into the crystal. With an alert and open mind allow yourself to feel its effects. Most people report a sensation of heat, a tingling or a pulsation. Try a few more crystals to see how different ones feel. The important thing is to go for the one which makes you feel more whole, more complete.

When choosing stones for others, simply visualise them and repeat the same process. This basic technique can be used for all crystals and gemstones.

CRYSTAL JEWELLERY

Wearing crystals as jewellery is both an effective and attractive way to utilise their healing properties or supply specific energies required to cope with life situations at home, work or in relationships. These stones are normally worn in the form of a pendant so that the crystal rests over the heart or thymus gland which controls the immune system.

Such stones can be chosen in exactly the same manner as already described for your clear crystal point. However this crystal will be on your person for much of the time and hence it's important to choose one which complements your energies. For example, people who worry a lot and suffer therefore from nervous tension and stress often find Amethyst is an excellent choice, and so on. The list of different stones and their properties given at the end of this book is a good guideline - but don't forget that the ultimate judge is your own intuitive instinct!

The practical use of crystals and gemstones to optimise life situations is a fascinating subject which we'll have to deal with in depth in volume 2; but we can take this opportunity to answer the most common questions about crystal jewellery.

The first question is whether the crystal should be worn pointing up or down. There's still some controversy over this, but the simple truth is that energy flows in whichever direction the crystal points and hence the decision rests with each individual's needs. A person whose energy is always "up in the clouds" may find a downward point a good way to ground that energy and focus their attention more on the level of physical reality, and vice versa. Double terminated crystals are now becoming more popular because they flow in both directions.

Of course, most of these double terminated crystals have been cut and polished, which brings us to the next question. Is it better to have a natural uncut crystal or not? The answer really lies in the cutting. So long as the crystal has been cut along its axis, i.e. in line with the helical spiral, then there's no problem.

In fact the crystal may have been enhanced since it's now more balanced around that axis. Obviously if the stone has been cut across its axis then its energy will be weakened - however I've found this is rarely the case. Besides, such a badly cut point would normally be felt and rejected during the selection procedure already given. On the other hand, a natural uncut crystal does retain its own unique character and inviduality, and so the whole question reduces to one of personal taste.

The last question is whether shapes other than the regular six sided point are effective. Basically we've found that spheres, pyramids, obelisks, cabochons, and even hearts are all useful in different ways. Faceted stones can also be useful if combined with a crystal point to direct their energy.

Whichever crystal you choose to wear it can be cleansed, opened and used for healing and visualisation as described.

CLEANSING YOUR CRYSTAL

The reason crystals work so well is that they both channel and store etheric or auric energies. Whenever anyone touches a crystal it immediately absorbs their energy pattern. So the crystal you've chosen actually carries the energies of all the people who've ever touched it!

To work with your crystal effectively the next step is to cleanse it of all those unwanted vibrations so that it only contains your own. We've listed below the six techniques we've found most effective. We recommend that every crystal you buy should be cleansed at least the first time by method 1 or 2.

1. Immerse the crystal in a jar of fresh OCEAN WATER. Sea water naturally absorbs the etheric energies in the crystal. This can take from 2 to 7 days depending on the size of the crystal and the energy it contains. If in any doubt, leave it the full 7 days. Throw away the water after use.

2. If you're too far from the sea buy some NATURAL SEA SALT from a health food shop. Don't add water, simply cover the crystal in dry salt and repeat as above.

3. Place the crystal in the EARTH, point up. This helps my pot plants flourish also! I find it particularly good for crystals which have picked up a tired or depleted energy pattern since it seems to regenerate them nicely as well as cleansing them.

4. Place the crystal on an AMETHYST CLUSTER, since this is a purifying stone. This is a very convenient method for the crystal that you wear, because you can simply place it on the cluster overnight (or maybe use method 3 if you had a particularly hard day!).

5. Using BREATH. This is an old Native American method. Holding the crystal upright in front of you, take a deep breath. Imagine yourself full of clear white light then blow sharply through the crystal, cleansing it of any extraneous vibrations.

6. A variation of the above is to hold the crystal between thumb and forefinger of the right hand. Inhale deeply, especially filling the upper chest. Then exhale very sharply through the nose, pulsing your awareness right through one face of the crystal and its opposite side. Repeat twice more, thus covering the three pairs of faces in three breaths.

The crystal is now cleansed of all vibrations except your own and will continue to "tune in" to you personally, thus working more effectively for you.

Once cleansed, it's best not to let anyone else touch your personal crystal and with some stones I apply this rule strictly. However in some circumstances it can be relaxed. For example, I knew one doctor in Tibet who left crystals with various healers so that he could use their vibration in his own healing. Jointly shared crystals can also enhance relationships, and so on.

Methods 5 and 6 are quick ways to cleanse your crystal if needed. Crystals also love to be left out in moonlight, which is polarised and charges them.

OPENING & PROGRAMMING YOUR CRYSTAL

Having chosen and cleansed your crystal, the next step is to make friends with it. To do this, choose a quiet time where there'll be no interruptions.

Sit down in a comfortable position and relax.

Take six or seven deep, deep breaths.

As you breathe in feel new energy and light entering your body.

Hold the breath for a moment, feeling full. As you exhale imagine any tensions or negativity you may be carrying flow out with the breath.

Take up your crystal in your left hand and hold it point up, resting over your heart chakra.

Breathe love, awareness, and light into the crystal. As you become aware of its presence ask it to release its healing energy, love and insight, for the highest benefit of yourself and others on the planet.

And so it's done. Both you and the crystal are ready to work together. Allow your breathing to return to its natural rhythm and bring your awareness back to your physical body and everyday reality.
In opening a crystal we also open ourselves in a conscious and loving manner. It's important to be aware in all crystal work

that there's a quality of sharing. The crystal contributes its own personality and energy, and you'll find this relationship deepens with time.

PROGRAMMING

Having opened our crystal we're now ready to work with it and programming our stone is a good way to start. A crystal can actually be programmed at any time but it's good practice in the beginning to do so after the opening exercise.

As we've seen, Quartz Crystal has the ability to amplify our personal energies and whilst these are subtle, their effect on our lives is powerful. Consider how strongly our moods, the whole range of emotions, the brightness of our thoughts and our feeling of physical well being affect our directions and levels of achievement. Quartz Crystal not only stimulates and clarifies those energies but also serves as a bridge by which we can consciously program them for desired effect.

Programming a crystal works in a similar way to affirmations, with two important differences. Firstly, because the crystal stimulates new levels of awareness which we can bring in to play, and secondly because we can utilise the ability of quartz to store vibrations, thoughts and visions to create a positive feedback system. In other words the crystal continually stimulates our whole being, rather than just our conscious mind, towards whatever goal we've chosen.

Programming Technique

1. Firstly build up a clear picture of your goal. Think of all the aspects which bear on it. If the goal involves other people then imagine the best possible conclusion for them also. For major manifestations, use the visualisation given later to seek more insight.

2. Either grip the crystal firmly, point up, in the right hand or hold it between the thumb and forefinger.

3. Visualising the goal as clearly as possible, project it into the crystal via a beam or spiral of white light emanating from the third eye. This is the crucial step, and results generally vary in direct proportion to the degree of totality or will with which you impress the crystal. To help this try to visualise with as many senses as possible: touch, taste, feelings, etc., so that the program leads to a very real feeling of success.

4. The crystal will now hold that program until such time as you either consciously erase it or overwrite it with a new one. Most small crystals need to be with you so that they're in direct contact with your energy.

Notes:

Only clear quartz can be programmed - other stones are already programmed by nature for specific purposes.

Very large or deep programs often need a larger crystal, possibly a free standing meditation crystal. This can be left at home, since it can work on your psyche from a distance. Such crystals can also be used by two or more people - a particularly nice start to relationships, for example, or for group meditations. In either case, the crystal can be programmed with group ideals, shared goals and so forth.

The crystal you wear can be readily reprogrammed throughout the day - this is very much like writing internal memos to yourself as different situations come up.

CRYSTAL VISUALISATION

Creative visualisation is already a popular and successful technique, and one to which crystals lend themselves particularly well. The crystal visualisation given can also be an essential part of programming in that we can use it to find out what we really want to program!

It's actually great fun inventing your own visualisations but we'll give you this one because after countless workshops it's proved the best way to enter your crystal and connect with its particular qualities.

The great advantage of visual thought is that in the process of it we can consciously let go of the verbal mind and hence perceive beyond its everyday reality. If you've ever had a strong dream whilst the logical mind sleeps and thus received a new insight into some current problem in your life, then you have an idea of how strong a tool visualisation can be.

Of course trying to visualise whilst the mind is awake is a different story, and hence the importance of relaxing body and mind as much as possible. If I had to describe visualisation in a few words, I'd say it's the art of being as close to the edge of sleep as possible - whilst remaining fully alert and awake! So for the following exercise choose a quiet comfortable space with minimum distractions.

1. Relax as before to the point where you're holding the crystal over your heart.

2. Visualise the crystal in your mind's eye, magnified in size and standing in a natural setting of your choice.

3. Imagine that there's a doorway set in one of its facets, and walk round the crystal until you find it.

4. Good, there it is. Now, if the door is closed, open it. It might just need a push, or maybe there's a handle or a button to press. Now enter your crystal. Just take a step inside.

5. Whilst on the threshold orientate yourself in this new space. What kind of light does it hold? Feel the walls and floor. Are they warm or cool? Take a deep breath. Does the air have a special smell?

6. Once you've accustomed yourself to this new environment, you notice a spiral staircase in front of you glowing in all the colours of the rainbow.

7. Slowly ascend this staircase towards the apex of the crystal. Feel your feet on each step as you're bathed in its colour ... first red, then orange, and so on....

8. Finally you step through the violet to the top of the stairs. Here you find a room occupied by the elemental guide of your crystal. This being sits in a comfortable chair and motions you to sit in the chair opposite which is equally comfortable.

9. Now you can greet the guide in whatever way seems suitable and begin a conversation. It's probably best to start by asking whether your guide has any special message for you, then you can ask any questions you came in with. Take as long for this as you want.

10. When the conversation is over either because the guide says so or because you feel yourself being pulled back to

your everyday reality, then thank you guide and descend the staircase, back through those glowing colours, to the door.

11. Leave through the same door, close it behind you and re-enter your physical body consciousness.

12. Take a few deep breaths, stretch your whole body; arms, back, legs, toes, etc.

13. Spend some time thinking about whatever you received. Some may like to keep a written record of the essence of each of these journeys. This is often good to refer back to and check out the actual quality of the information given.

Notes:

This particular visualisation is powerful because the spiral staircase represents the actual flow of energy within a crystal and the colours relate to your chakras. So we're actually "climbing up" from our physical reality to higher realms.

Anything which occurs in such an exercise has meaning. For example you may have found the door locked, hard to push, or rusted. So look at how you may make it hard for yourself to open up to new ideas or new people in reality.

Exercises like these are fine examples of how we can use crystals to integrate our rational and intuitive sides. A rational mind sets up the visualisation and asks the questions. But the guide we meet we can only sense intuitively because we don't consciously create his form nor his answers, which is the whole point of it!
In fact, my basic test of the validity of these exercises is if they reach a point where I suddenly realise that the answers I'm get-

ting aren't predictable; in fact they contain information and insights which are not only new to me but also carry that unmistakable ring of truth.

Also, don't worry if you can't visualise everything perfectly. The less you TRY the better it works! It's best to focus on "going with the flow". So maybe your guide didn't look as old and wise or young and beautiful as you expected. That's OK - the form is part of the message also!

CRYSTAL HEALING - THE ENERGY BODY

As we mentioned in the introduction, the basis of crystal healing is the interaction between the energy of the crystal and that of the human body.

Looking at the human energy field more closely we see that there are seven main energy centres or chakras, within it. As you can see from the diagram and following list, these aren't at all mysterious. Each relates to an obvious set of emotions and feelings which from this viewpoint simply represent different energy levels, or aspects of consciousness. They also relate to different glands by which the body controls our hormones, and hence our energy levels, emotional states, etc.

Ideally, energy should be able to flow naturally and freely between all these centres and this would represent a state of health and well being. But wherever that natural flow of energy is blocked for too long then physical illness ultimately arises.

Unfortunately, the latter is generally the case. Over the course of our lives we have built up a whole set of preconditioned reactions and responses which interfere with that natural flow.

In the healing techniques which follow we show how to use clear quartz and other stones to remedy that situation. The strength of a crystal healing lies in the fact that we can by-pass those psychological blocks and heal the energy body directly. In doing so we also stimulate the body's own natural healing processes, and these are by no means insignificant. After all, your body is the product of millenia of evolution in which the development of such a self-healing instinct had, and has, a tremendously high survival value.

In these forms of healing the power of love has always been a vital factor - but there's a reason here for the scientific mind also. Just above the heart sits the thymus gland which controls the immune system. Hence a loving person, one who is in touch with the needs of their heart, is a healthy person!

This concept of the chakra system has long been a fact of life in the East but is fast gaining popularity in the West because it offers a much more lucid and comprehensive insight into human nature on many levels. We have made one change however.

Most Eastern sources refer to only seven main chakras. Whilst this is correct according to the physical glands in our body to which these chakras relate, western society has a different psychology. It's much more mentally disciplined and this creates tension for the intuitive and playful child within us. So we've divided the plexus area into two by counting the navel as a centre in its own right.

In the following listing of the chakras the stones given are all quartz based, these being generally the most powerful and by virtue of being in the same family their energies blend together particularly well.

Due to its colour, each vibrates at a different level and hence stimulates a different centre, in the same way that different colours affect our overall psychological state. The reason for this is that an over abundance of one colour vibrates its particular chakra/energy level more than the others. A richly coloured gemstone is a potent and alive source of that colour vibration.

HUMAN ENERGY SYSTEM
THE CHAKRAS & THEIR RELEVANT GLANDS

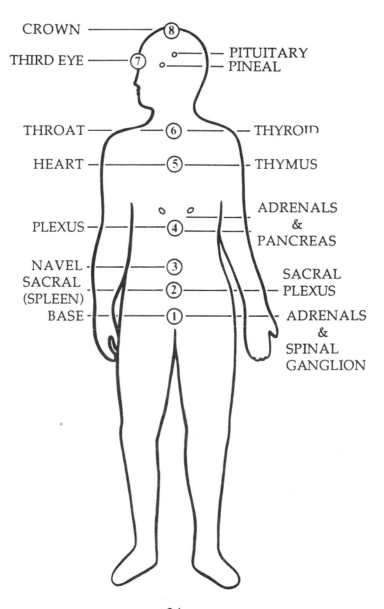

CROWN ——— ⑧

THIRD EYE ——— ⑦   ——— PITUITARY
                              ——— PINEAL

THROAT ——— ⑥ ——— THYROID

HEART ——— ⑤ ——— THYMUS

                              ADRENALS
                                 &
PLEXUS ——— ④ ——— PANCREAS

NAVEL ——— ③
SACRAL ——— ②   SACRAL
(SPLEEN)   ——— PLEXUS

BASE ——— ①   ——— ADRENALS
                                 &
                              SPINAL
                              GANGLION

THE CHAKRAS AND THEIR STONES

1. BASE CHAKRA (black)

Located at base of spine: Place stone on centre of pubic bone, this chakra relates to the physical body and the "fight or flight" reaction.

The stone is SMOKY QUARTZ which brings white light (i.e. pure consciousness) into the physical and is good for regaining life enthusiasm, overcoming depression, etc. It can "short circuit" emotional or mental problems which drain our energy simply by pulling our awareness back into the physical body.

2. SACRAL (SPLEEN) CHAKRA (red-orange)

Place stone midway between base chakra and navel. This is the creativity chakra in all areas; creating children is but one way to use this energy.

The stone is CARNELIAN - activating, revitalising and regenerating. It's excellent for strengthening the liver and overcoming lethargy.

3. NAVEL CENTRE (orange-yellow)

Place stone on or just below navel. Here we are dealing with desires and their fulfilment - the umbilical cord, the child within us. The navel connects us to life, to personal nourishment, and to our innocence. So the stone is CITRINE, a golden yellow channelling the energy of the sun - warming, comforting, energising and life giving.

4. SOLAR PLEXUS CENTRE (green)

This is situated just below the point where our ribs part. The plexus is personal power. It controls breath, by which we can energise ourselves and focus the navel energy more consciously. It's our primal ego, the sense of the powerful self, and hence is also the main area of emotional congestion and frustration.

So the stone is GREEN AVENTURINE - the all round healer - which helps to release trauma from the mental, emotional and physical bodies, relaxing the tensions we feel in this area.

5. HEART CHAKRA (pink)

Situated in the centre of the chest this is compassion, love, understanding, feeling and wisdom. The stone is ROSE QUARTZ which brings that energy within in a loving way, emphasising self love and self healing. So often we "hurt" on this level because we love others more easily than we do ourselves.

The thymus gland which controls the immune system, is also situated here, showing us the importance of love in healing.

6. THROAT CHAKRA (sky blue)

This is situated in the nook at the base of the neck, it's to do with sound, rhythm, vibration and communication. How we creatively express the truth we see and feel. Containing the thyroid as it does, it affects our whole body energy.

The stone here is BLUE LACE AGATE: having a light energy which cools, clear and clarifies our ideas for communication.

7. THIRD EYE (violet purple)
Positioned between and just above the eyebrows, this is the centre of inner vision, intuition and higher or spiritual mind. This

is where we actively focus our mental and intuitive energy.

The stone is AMETHYST, the purple ray, which initiates intuition. It also de-stresses the nervous sytem and stimulates spiritual awareness.

8. CROWN CHAKRA (clear white)

Located in top of the head - the fontanelle, the first part of our body to see the world. This is our connection to universal consciousness - moving beyond the sense of individual self which sees the centres separately to a state of being which contains and integrates them all.

The stone is CLEAR QUARTZ which generates a dynamic white light comprised of all the colours of the rainbow. This means that it contains the vibrations of all the chakras.

CRYSTAL HEALING TECHNIQUES

It's best to practice these on yourself at first so that you can feel the effects of the crystal energy directly. The crystal is simply moving your energy. When working over the heart area that energy will be felt as emotional. Over the brow area it may be felt as mental tension, etc. The reason we use clear quartz, the predominant healing stone, is that it generates a dynamic white light which contains all the colours of the rainbow and hence the chakra system, so it can be used everywhere.

Once you're familiar with the effects of crystal energy on your own system then you can start on other people. Often in such work you can accelerate or bring on a 'Healing Crisis'. Working over the heart area for example may cause tears to flow as old emotional pain is brought to the surface to be released. In such moments simply allow yourself or your partner to let go and release that pain lovingly.

In this book we're giving a lot information in a very small space. The reason we're doing so is because we place great faith in your intuitive awareness, as we do in ours.

The point is that our intuitive sense is the one which naturally perceives in terms of energy, and hence sees a much more complete picture than the logical mind which can only perceive one thing at a time. This is why intuition is so often right even when it's wrong! So long as you're moving from a state of love, awareness and sensitivity to the other person your intuition won't let you down. It's important not to lose touch with whoever you're working on.

Before we go into any healing, it's helpful to connect to the stones.

Just relax and hold each one in your left hand and feel its energy. Be aware how it leads your thoughts and feelings in a certain direction.

It's important to be receptive and relaxed since crystal energy is subtle and the effort of trying too hard can eclipse the effects.

SINGLE CRYSTAL HEALING

This is the basic healing technique, involving just one clear crystal.

1. Relax and tune in to your crystal as described in the section on opening crystals. This is a good meditation to do before any healing work. Take all the time you need in the beginning, you'll find it gets much easier and quicker with practice.

2. Holding the crystal by the base in your right hand, play the point (through which the crystal energy moves) over the palm of your left hand. You should be able to feel a sensation of warmth or a tingling as you did when choosing a crystal. (In fact, I often use this as an alternative and quick way to choose a crystal). If you find trouble with this then warm the crystal up by rotating it briskly between the palms of your hands and try again.

3. Move the crystal to any part of your body feeling pain or tension or just that it needs some attention.

4. Rotate the crystal point over that area in a circular motion.

You'll probably find that either clockwise or anti-clockwise direction feels best. Follow that feeling. After a while you may reverse that direction if it feels right to do so.

5. When the hand naturally comes to a rest, the healing is complete, or your hand holding the crystal may wish to move to another area and cleanse that in the same way.

6. Spend a few minutes quietly feeling the changes that have taken place during the healing.

CHAKRA BALANCING

1. Sitting comfortably relaxed, hold your crystal in your right hand as in previous method.

2. Start with the crystal over the crown chakra, point towards it, and rotate over that centre. If you can feel the effect, allow the crystal to follow its natural motion. Otherwise, visualise white light pouring into that centre.

3. After a few minutes move down to the next chakra, repeat the process, then down to the next until you've covered all of them.

4. To complete this general energy healing sit for a few more moments visualising white light flowing into your crown, down through the soles of the feet into the earth.

AURA CLEANSING

This technique revitalizes, cleanses and balances the whole energy system. The aura is the electromagnetic energy field which surrounds the human body and indicates its total state of health.

You can feel someone's aura quite easily just by relaxing your awareness into the left hand and starting perhaps a few feet away move it slowly closer to their body. At a certain point - it's quite a clear boundary - one feels a band of warmth. One can also run the left hand over someone's body in the same way, feeling localised intensities where energy is blocked and needs moving. This is useful for step 5 in the single crystal healing to locate areas that need working on. Simply hold the crystal (already opened to our love) over that area to actively give the healing.

The left hand is the receptive intuitive hand since it connects to the right side of the brain which controls our intuitive functions. The right hand is the active giving one since it connects to the rational left brain.

Method

For this technique you need:

a). a partner
b). 3 or 4 crystals. Clear crystals are often called male or fire crystals because of the dynamic nature of their energy.
c). 2 milky crystals. These are generally called feminine because their energy is more soft and nurturing.

1. Ask your partner to lie down on his/her back, palms up, and help him/her to relax using the breath as before.

2. Place other crystals in the following positions:
   a clear crystal over the crown, point down, to bring light into the body;
   a female crystal at his/her feet, point upwards, to draw earth energy into the body;
   a female crystal in the left hand, point up;
   a male crystal, point down, in his/her right hand.

3. Take another clear crystal and place it on any area needing special attention. Point down if that area needs grounding, point up if it needs uplift and expansion.

4. Ask how your partner is feeling. If he/she reports any tension, ask them to breathe into that spot, releasing and relaxing it.

5. Holding a clear crystal in your right hand, rotate it over the chakras as the chakra balancing, breathing in love

and light until the chakra system feels cleared and balanced.

6. Moving the crystal back up to the crown, visualise your partner's aura as an egg shape round the body, perhaps two to six inches away from it.

7. Now we can begin to scrub the aura. To do this use the same rotating action, starting from the crown and moving down the right hand side to the feet, then back up the left side ending again in the crown, covering the whole surface area of the aura.

   Whilst this is happening, tell your partner he/she can just drift away and float with any feelings, daydreams or other images which may arise. These often bring useful insights into patterns which create tension, etc.

8. Once you've finished give your partner a countdown from 5 to 1, bringing their consciousness back into his/her physical body and everyday reality. Remove the stones and have a cup of tea!

FULL STONE LAYOUT

The basic difference between this and previous methods is that here we use different coloured gemstones which generate the specific vibrations of each chakra, and hence each is recharged and revitalised. It's also good in that we can "tune in" to the different qualities of these stones. This means that if we need any particular energy during the day, we know which stone to wear or carry with us.

The other difference is that here we're using a simple guided visualisation. It's good not to give yourself a hard time trying to get it perfect. The FEELING of golden white light flowing through you is quite good enough!

You can also combine this layout with the previously described techniques, particularly using a single point to focus on areas needing special attention.

THE HEALING

Choose a quiet space where you can feel comfortable. It's good to do this for fifteen minutes, morning and evening.

Lie down on your back, palms up, head on a pillow (on which you can position the crown stone).

Take a few deep breaths, exhaling any tensions.

Maintaining a relaxed state, place the stones one by one on your body in their respective positions, by referring to the list given.

When they are all placed, relax a little more deeply and allow the breath to find a steady rhythm.

Starting from the crown, breathe the colour vibration of each stone into its chakra, spending a few minutes on each. This will allow a deeper penetration of the subtle bodies.

Then on each inhalation visualise or imagine a stream of white light entering the crown, travelling down through each chakra.

As the light touches each chakra feel it begin to spin, igniting its colour brightly.

On each exhalation visualise the white light flowing back up the spine and out through the crown.

Once all the chakras are ignited allow the colours to join, forming a brilliant rainbow.

With each breath feel the rainbow energy nourishing your body.

Continue breathing regularly and relaxing until you feel the system achieving balance.

When that is achieved, stay with it a little longer, so you can remember how it feels. Then remove the stones in the order you feel right.

Cleanse them by washing them lovingly under running water and put them in a special place. It's good to keep them in the bag on an amethyst cluster since this is a purifier.

OTHER HEALING STONES

This book has concentrated on clear quartz since its great versatility makes it easily the most important healing stone. Yet nature has also provided a wide range of other stones, each of which offers special qualities which can also be used in healing. These stones are more specific in their use. Each one reflects or amplifies a different aspect of your being.

They can be opened and tuned into in much the same way as already described for clear quartz.

AMETHYST: Quartz coloured purple by minute traces of iron.
Qualities: Refer chakra list.

APOPHYLLITE: A silicate, often seen as brilliant green 'castles' having four sides and a terminating point.
Qualities: This is a very uplifting stone, clearing the central energy channel which connects all the chakras. Working particularly well in opening the Crown, the third eye, and the higher aspects of the heart, it facilitates the connection to higher self and hence universal intelligence.

AQUAMARINE: A type of beryl, having a transparent pale blue colour.
Qualities: Gently opening the throat, this stone connects our thoughts and emotions and clarifies inner and outer communication.

AVENTURINE: Green quartz often spangled with flecks of mica.
Qualities: Refer chakra list.

BLOODSTONE: An opaque iron oxide which often forms beautiful abstracts of greens, reds, pinks and browns.
Qualities: Marvellously warm and calming to hold, this stone serves to strengthen circulation and to detoxify the blood.

CARNELIAN: Chalcedony quartz, coloured red-orange by minute traces of hematite.
Qualities: Refer list of chakras.

CITRINE: Quartz, coloured yellow or brown by inclusion of iron hydrates.
Qualities: Refer list of chakras.

CHRYSOPRASE: Translucent chalcedony quartz coloured apple green by traces of nickel.
Qualities: Vibrates and awakens the psychic body.

GARNET: Translucent red.
Qualities: Pulses, realigns and energises the lower chakras, thus helping to regenerate the body.

HEMATITE: An iron oxide generally seen as tumbled stones which have a beautiful silvery polish.
Qualities: In many ways similar to bloodstone, hematite also brings out inner strength on the physical plane - the 'iron in the soul'.

LAPIS LAZULI: Deep blue and opaque, the best samples having tiny flecks of golden iron pyrites scattered through them.
Qualities: Sometimes known as the "Messenger of Heaven" this stone has been prized through the ages for its ability to calmly cut through our unconscious blocks and reveal the intuitive sense of self. Suspending judgements and awakening a deep inner silence, it's an excellent stone for meditation.

MALACHITE: Coloured green by the presence of copper, this soft opaque stone often has beautiful bandings which make it popular for jewellery.
Qualities: Releases suppressed emotions, particularly those related to areas where we limit our power. It presents a very down to earth mirror to inspect ourselves in.

OBSIDIAN: Essentially a black volcanic glass.
Qualities: This is not a stone to be taken lightly, since the energy it generates cuts through conscious thought patterns revealing whatever lies beneath. This makes it useful in breaking down old conditioned patterns which restrict us but it does do so in quite a confronting way.

ROSE QUARTZ: Coloured pink by minute traces of manganese or titanium.
Qualities: Refer to list of chakras.

SMOKY QUARTZ: Coloured light brown to black (known as morion).
Qualities: Refer to list of chakras.

TURQUOISE: A light blue soft and opaque stone.
Qualities: Amplifies healing energy. Strengthens and focuses mental communication. A good stone to wear for general physical health.

TOURMALINE: This group of silicates is translucent to transparent, ranging in colour from black through green, pink, blue and gold.
Qualities: As tourmaline is even more piezoelectric than quartz, energy flows along it very rapidly, making it an excellent cleanser. It's particularly good for transmuting physical blocks into energy. The different colours apply to different areas.

Pink Tourmaline - cleanses and energises the heart, facilitating its expression.

Green Tourmaline - a cleanser of emotional and physical blocks, manifesting power in a very clear way by bringing previously unconscious energies into awareness.

Watermelon Tourmaline - perhaps the most sought after combination, being green on the outside and pink on the inside it combines the above two in a tremendously positive way, enabling us to achieve a state of personal power combined with emotional clarity.

There are, of course, many other stones, and much more to say about those described above. Look for the second volume of the Practical Guide to Crystal Healing which will explore these stones in much more depth.

We hope you've enjoyed this brief journey into the world of crystals and that they become as much a part of your lives as they have ours.

Remember, a crystal lasts forever and can continue to bring its light into your life for years to come.

NOTES